Girls and Goddesses

For Mirren and Gowan.
Be your own heroines.

Text copyright © 2013 Lari Don
Illustrations copyright © 2013 Francesca Greenwood
This translation of *Girls and Goddesses* is published by Darby Creek by
arrangement with Bloomsbury Publishing Plc.

Darby Creek
A division of Lerner Publishing Group, Inc.
241 First Avenue North
Minneapolis, MN 55401 USA

For reading levels and more information, look up this title at
www.lernerbooks.com.

Main body text set in Sabon LT Std 13/19.
Typeface provided by Adobe Systems.

Library of Congress Cataloging-in-Publication Data

Names: Don, Lari, author. | Greenwood, Francesca, illustrator.
Title: Girls and goddesses : stories of heroines from around the world / by
     Lari Don ; illustrations by Francesca Greenwood.
Description: Minneapolis : Darby Creek, [2016] | Series: World of stories |
     Audience: Age: 7–12. | Audience: Grade 4 to 6.
Identifiers: LCCN 2015046658| ISBN 9781512413175 (lb : alk. paper) |
     ISBN 9781512413373 (pb : alk. paper)
Subjects: LCSH: Women heroes—Folklore—Juvenile literature.
Classification: LCC GR515 .D66 2016 | DDC 398.2—dc23

LC record available at http://lccn.loc.gov/2015046658

Manufactured in the United States of America
1 – SB – 7/15/16

Girls and Goddesses

STORIES OF HEROINES FROM AROUND THE WORLD

LARI DON

Illustrated by
Francesca Greenwood

MINNEAPOLIS

Contents

Chi and the
Seven-Headed Dragon
Chinese legend

Dragons can be awkward neighbors, so when the Emperor of China saw a dragon settle into the cave at the top of the mountain behind his palace, he wasn't pleased.

It was the biggest, scariest dragon he'd ever seen. It had seven heads, on seven snaky necks, attached to one thick, green, scaly body, and each individual head had ninety-nine sharp,

curved yellow teeth. (I'm sure *you* can work out how many teeth the dragon had altogether, but the Emperor didn't bother doing the math. He just knew it was far too many teeth.)

"I can't have a dragon living above my palace!" he whined. "If it comes out of that cave, it might fly down here, frighten my party guests, and set fire to my palace. It might even eat me!"

He summoned his wise men and his wise women, and he asked them, "How do we get rid of that dragon?"

The wise men and wise women frowned. "It's not easy to get rid of a dragon, oh great Emperor, but we could make sure it doesn't leave its cave, then it wouldn't threaten your palace."

"How would we do that?" demanded the Emperor.

"If we feed the dragon its favorite food at the mouth of the cave, then it won't need to leave the cave."

"Great idea," said the Emperor. "What is its favorite food?"

The wise men and wise women looked a bit embarrassed, so the Emperor stamped his feet

until they admitted that the long, green, seven-headed dragon's favorite food was:

Little girls.

"Little girls?" said the Emperor. "Little *girls*? But I can't feed little girls to the dragon! I don't want to feed my own daughters to it, and I don't want to feed the daughters of my cooks or soldiers or gardeners or civil servants to it either, because then they wouldn't like me and they wouldn't work for me."

The wise men and wise women said, "There are lots of farmers, fishermen, and merchants outside your palace who have daughters. You could feed their little girls to the dragon to keep it safely in the cave."

So the Emperor demanded a silk bag filled with the names of all the families in China who didn't work in his palace, and every Friday morning he picked out a name. Then a messenger on a fast horse rode to that family and announced in a loud, shouty voice:

"By order of the Emperor, you must feed one of your little girls to the seven-headed dragon. But because the Emperor is kind and merciful,

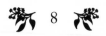

you may choose which of your daughters to give to the dragon."

So each week, a family would take a little girl up the mountain. They would all walk up a steep, winding path to the very top, where they would sit the little girl outside the cave, then bang a big brass gong put there by the Emperor's servants. The *booommmmm* of the gong told the dragon that his tea was ready. Then the family would go away.

Leaving the little girl on the mountain to be eaten.

Over weeks and months and years, the steep path to the summit got wider, trodden down by the many feet which had climbed up and the fewer feet which had walked slowly and sadly back down.

But it worked! It worked perfectly, from the Emperor's point of view, because the dragon stayed in the cave and didn't bother him at all.

Then one Friday, the name he pulled out of the bag was Li, a rice farmer. So the

messenger rode to Li's rice farm and said in a bored voice:

"By order of the Emperor, you must feed one of your little girls to the seven-headed dragon. But because the Emperor is kind and merciful, *you* may choose which of your daughters to give to the dragon."

Li looked at his three lovely daughters with tears in his eyes.

His youngest daughter, whose name was Chi, thought this was a dreadful thing to ask any father to do, to choose one of his children to feed to a dragon.

So, to save her father from making such a terrible choice and to save her big sisters from the dragon, Chi said, "I will go. I will go and meet the dragon. But I would like to ask three favors of you, Father. I'd like to take the sword that hangs over the fireplace, I'd like you to give me seven barrels of your best sticky rice, and I'd like to go up the mountain on my own."

The next morning, Chi left the farm with a long sword in her belt, pulling behind her a cart loaded with seven barrels of sticky rice.

As she walked up the mountain on her own, she could smell the rice. Her father had cooked the sticky rice before he put it in the barrels, so as she pulled the cart, she was surrounded by the warm, sweet, toasty smell of cooked rice. She knew the rice in the barrels was gluey, gloopy, and glutinous.

When she got to the top of the mountain, she placed the seven barrels of rice in a line at the mouth of the cave, hid herself and the cart behind the big gong, then banged the gong to tell the dragon his tea was ready.

The dragon's heads came out of the cave.

Seven huge heads appeared out of the darkness, with ninety-nine sharp teeth in each head. Seven long necks followed, weaving and winding around each other, as the heavy body squatted in the cave.

Seven heads on seven necks, hunting for a meal.

Each head had to pass over a barrel of rice as it came out of the cave. And each head smelled the rice—the warm, toasty, sweet-scented sticky rice.

The dragon's favorite food *was* little girls. However, it had eaten nothing but little girls for years now. The dragon breathed in the fragrance of the rice and thought, "That smells good. I could have rice for a starter and a little girl for the main course."

So the seven heads dove . . . one, two, three, four, five, six, seven . . . into the seven barrels of rice and started to eat.

As soon as all seven heads were in the seven barrels, Chi grasped the hilt of the sword and ran at the dragon.

The dragon heard her coming and the dragon attacked with its first three heads.

But the first, second, and third heads were so deep in the barrels of sticky rice that they couldn't get out. They were stuck in the barrels.

So Chi ran up to the first three heads and CHOP CHOP CHOP she cut them off.

The next three heads attacked.

The fourth, fifth, and sixth heads hadn't gone so deep into the rice, because they had started eating after the first three heads, so

they managed to pull themselves out of the barrels of sticky rice and started chasing Chi around the mountaintop.

But those three heads had eaten lots of rice, so when they tried to bite her with their ninety-nine teeth each, there was so much sticky rice on their teeth and gums that they couldn't open their mouths. Their jaws were stuck together.

Chi realized they couldn't bite her, so she whirled around and CHOP CHOP CHOP she cut off those three heads too.

But the seventh head had gone into the rice last, and by the time it had snaked into the seventh barrel, the dragon's belly was almost full from the rice eaten by the other six heads.

The seventh head hadn't gone very deep, so it pulled out of the barrel clean and fast. And the seventh head hadn't eaten very much, so its teeth weren't stuck together.

When the seventh head started to chase Chi, the seventh head opened its mouth wide and Chi saw the ninety-nine long, yellow teeth.

So Chi ran away.

As she crouched behind the gong, she thought, "I had planned to fight a dragon with all its heads and teeth stuck in rice. I hadn't planned to fight a dragon with ninety-nine teeth snapping at me!" And she looked at the path down the mountain.

Then she thought, "Hold on, I've just fought a seven-headed dragon. This is only a *one*-headed dragon!"

She leaped out from behind the gong. She jumped onto a barrel of rice. She waited until the dragon's head snaked toward her.

And she sliced its head off.

Then Chi kicked the barrels down the mountain, to roll down the slope and thud into the back wall of the palace, and she kicked the dragon's heads down the mountain, to bounce down the slope and squelch into the back wall of the palace.

Because she thought that since the Emperor had happily fed little girls to the dragon for so long, he should clear up the mess.

Inanna and
the Box of Monsters
Sumerian myth

Inanna was the Sumerian goddess of love, so she was glamorous and popular, but not as powerful as the rest of her family. She had often wondered how she could gain more power and influence.

Her uncle, Enki, was the god of the sea and the god of wisdom, so he had all the world's skills and knowledge hoarded in his palace, far out to sea.

Inanna decided to pay her favorite uncle a visit.

She polished her ax and her sword, she put on her most flattering robe and richest jewels, and she left her home city of Uruk with her sidekick, Ninshibur. Ninshibur was a queen and a warrior, but she had chosen to serve as Inanna's chamberlain.

The two young women left the inland city of Uruk for the nearest harbor, where Inanna kept the boat of heaven, her beautiful, white, crescent-shaped boat. The boat of heaven was lit by two round oil lamps, one hanging from the front so Inanna and Ninshibur could see where they were going, the other hanging from the back so they could see where they had been.

Inanna and Ninshibur jumped into the boat of heaven, and they rowed across the wide water to Enki's sea-washed palace.

Well, I say *they* rowed, but Inanna was a goddess, so she just sat in the back of the boat and trailed her fingers in the water, while Ninshibur did all the hard work with the oars.

Eventually they arrived at Enki's palace. The god of wisdom and of the sea rarely had visitors because he lived so far from land, and he was delighted to see Inanna. He ordered his chamberlain, Isimud, to prepare a feast. Isimud opened up the feasting hall, which was filled with carved wooden boxes, and laid the long table with barley cakes, butter, honey, and beer.

Enki sat at one end with Isimud standing behind him. Inanna sat at the other end with Ninshibur standing behind her.

And they feasted.

Inanna was the perfect guest. When Enki told jokes she laughed, when he sang songs she joined in with the chorus, when he told stories she gasped in all the right places.

Then it was her turn and Inanna started to sing. She sang a long, gentle, quiet song.

Enki's face grew soft and his eyes started to droop. He said to her, in between verses, "Thank you so much for coming to visit me . . . I'm so happy to see you at my table . . . what can I give you to say thank you for visiting?"

Inanna kept singing, her voice smooth and low, and Enki looked around his feasting hall. He saw the carved, wooden boxes, holding all his knowledge, skills, and ideas.

Inanna kept singing her persuasively beautiful song. The god of wisdom staggered over to the boxes and started throwing open the lids. Inside the boxes, he saw crafts like woodworking and metalworking, he saw ideas like kingship and heroism.

"Here's a gift to say thanks for visiting your lonely old uncle," he said, as he gave the craft of the coppersmith to Inanna. But Inanna didn't stop singing, she just smiled sweetly and passed the gift to Ninshibur behind her, who slipped out of the hall and hid the gift in the boat of heaven.

Enki kept opening boxes and kept giving Inanna gifts as she sang. He gave her crowns and swords; colored clothes and black clothes; the loud music of instruments and the sad music of lamentation; the art of hairdressing and the craft of the scribe; the idea of shepherds' huts and sheep pens; good judgment and good

counsel; forthright speech and fancy speech and deceitful speech.

Isimud tried to stop Enki, but Enki ordered him to sit down and be quiet.

As Inanna sang, the god of wisdom opened every box he could see. He smiled at Inanna and gave her every gift he could find. And Ninshibur stowed the gifts in the boat of heaven.

Finally, Inanna changed to an even slower, softer song, and Enki fell gently asleep at the table.

Inanna and Ninshibur ran to the boat of heaven. They leaped in and they started to row away from the palace toward Uruk.

Well, I say *they* rowed, but Inanna was a goddess, so she just sat at the back of the boat and let her fingers dangle in the water, while Ninshibur did all the hard work with the oars.

Before they were even half-way home, Enki woke up. He rubbed his eyes, he shook his head, and he looked around his hall.

He saw the empty boxes.

Enki yelled at Isimud, "Where is my wisdom? Where is everything? All the crafts and knowledge and ideas?"

"You gave everything away, my lord. To your niece Inanna."

"I gave it all away? Go and get it back!"

So Isimud leaped into the sea god's fastest boat and he chased after the boat of heaven. When he caught up, he bowed to Inanna and said politely, "This is a little awkward, my lady, but my lord would like his gifts back. He didn't really mean to give them to you. So please return them."

Inanna smiled. "The god of wisdom wants his gifts back? Because he didn't mean to give them to me? That must mean the god of wisdom made a mistake. Not very *wise*, is he? Perhaps these crafts, ideas, and knowledge are safer with me. So no, he can't have them back."

Ninshibur rowed on, away from Isimud.

Isimud rushed back to Enki. "She's not going to return your gifts, no matter how politely I ask."

Enki smiled. "Then we will just have to take them back." He reached into a shadowy corner and dragged out a box which he hadn't noticed the night before.

"This," he said, "is the box of monsters."

He lifted the lid carefully, stuck his hand inside and hauled out an enkum, a wild-haired creature.

He said to the creature of the water, "Bring everything back to me!" and threw the enkum into the sea.

The enkum swam as fast as the waves after the boat of heaven.

The wild-haired enkum was blue, like the sea on a sunny day, and covered in long hair all over his body, on his head, his arms, his hands, his fingers, his belly, his knees, his feet. His hair was wiry and curly, and wound around anything near the enkum. It even wound around the enkum's own body, the hairs of his head twisting and twining and growing into his ears and up his nostrils.

When he reached the boat of heaven, his hair coiled around the oars so Ninshibur

couldn't row. Inanna laughed. "I'll deal with this." She picked up her ax and her sword, and she hacked at the enkum's hair with her ax and slashed at his belly with her sword.

But the ax bounced off his hair and the sword couldn't pierce his skin.

Inanna looked at her hands, dripping wet from trailing in the sea. She yelled to Ninshibur, "My hands have touched Enki's sea, so my hands have no power against his monsters. You will have to fight the enkum yourself, Ninshibur, because your hands have not touched the sea."

Ninshibur looked at the wild-haired enkum behind the boat, and she looked at the lamps fore and aft. She seized the nearest lamp and threw it at the enkum.

The lamp hit him square in the middle of his forehead. The lamp smashed open, burning oil splattered all over the enkum, and his hair caught fire. The flames rushed up each spiral hair and covered his body in a blaze of light.

The fire traveled along his hair, into his ears, up his nostrils, and right inside his

head. The enkum was burning inside and out, and he slowly sank, sizzling, under the waves.

Ninshibur started to row toward land.

But Enki opened the box of monsters again, stuck his hand inside, and hauled out a kugulal.

He said to the creature of the air, "Bring back everything," and threw the kugulal upward.

The kugulal flew as fast as the wind after the boat of heaven.

The kugulal was a huge bird, with a massive, deep breast, because the kugulal's weapon was not her beak nor her talons, but her voice. The kugulal had one huge lung in her chest, which gave so much power and volume to her call that she could shatter buildings and drive people mad.

The kugulal flew over the boat of heaven, shrieking and squealing. Inanna and Ninshibur had to cover their ears because the piercing noise was unbearable. As Ninshibur crouched down, trying to get away from the bird's screams, she could see the boat begin to shake apart under her feet.

She pulled her fingers out of her ears, and with her own body quivering and jerking in the waves of sound, she ran her nails between the boards of the boat to scrape up some of the bitumen which made it waterproof. Then she stuck the bitumen in her ears, to block out the noise so she could move and think.

Ninshibur grabbed Inanna's sword, stood up tall, and drove the sword straight above her head, right into the breast of the kugulal. The blade ripped open the bird's lung and suddenly the only noise the kugulal could make was a sad whistle as the air leaked out of her chest.

The kugulal turned and flapped slowly home.

And Ninshibur rowed toward the coast.

Enki had sent a creature of the water and a creature of the air, so next he sent creatures of the earth.

As they neared the shore, Inanna and Ninshibur saw fifty uru giants: giants so tall that their faces were hidden in the clouds, giants so big their footprints were valleys in the earth.

The giants were standing at the harbor.

Ninshibur said, "I will do anything for you, my lady Inanna, but I don't think even I can defeat fifty uru giants with just an ax and a sword. So I don't think we can land the boat at the harbor."

Inanna looked at the giants, at the harbor, at the roofs of her city a few miles inland, and said, "I don't think we need to land."

"But how else can we get the gifts to the city?"

Inanna smiled and put her fingers back in the water. Then she pushed the water, Enki's own water, toward the shore.

The seawater rose and poured over the shore, over the harbor and toward the city. The giants, being creatures of the land, moved away from the water.

The water flooded Uruk. Not like a tidal wave, but like a jug carefully filling a glass. Water slipped into the streets, filling them gently to turn them into calm canals.

Ninshibur kept rowing past the flooded harbor, as Inanna waved cheerfully at the

retreating giants.

The people of Uruk stood on tables, window sills, and roofs to watch their goddess and her boat of heaven move across the new wider sea toward the city, then float along the streets.

The boat floated toward Inanna's temple, where she and her gifts would be safe until Enki's anger and the seawater subsided.

Inanna and Ninshibur reached the temple steps, they unpacked the gifts, and they carried them into the temple.

Well, I say *they* unpacked the gifts, but Inanna was a goddess, so she raised her arms and acknowledged the cheers of her people, while Ninshibur did all the heavy lifting.

That is how Inanna brought all the arts and knowledge of civilization to people, not just the people of Uruk, but all the people of the world. That is how Inanna become the most powerful goddess of her time.

With a little help from her sidekick, Ninshibur.

The Wolf in the Bed
French Folktale

O nce there was a young girl who lived at the edge of the forest.

On baking day, her mother said to the girl, "I've baked an extra loaf. Why don't you take some fresh bread to your granny in the forest?"

So the girl placed a warm loaf of bread in her basket, wrapped herself in her bright colorful cloak, and said goodbye to her mother.

Then she began to walk to her granny's little cottage in the middle of the forest. She walked along a narrow path, through the dark shadows of the trees. Soon she came to a fork in the path, one straight path leading directly to her granny's cottage, the other path winding the long way around.

By the fork in the path, she saw a young man leaning against a tree. He had long hair, yellow eyes, long fingernails, and gleaming white teeth.

"Where are you going, young lady?" he asked.

"I'm off to visit my granny, to take her a loaf of fresh bread."

She showed him the bread in the basket. He leaned forward, toward the loaf and the girl's hand holding the basket, and he breathed in deeply. "What a wonderful smell."

"Would you like me to tear off a bit of crust for you? I'm sure Granny wouldn't mind."

"No, thank you. I don't want to spoil my appetite before dinner." He grinned, then asked, "So which path will you take?"

She laughed. "I'll take the straight, short path, of course."

"Then I hope you travel safely through the forest."

The girl said goodbye politely and walked along the straight path.

As soon as she was out of sight, the young man dropped to the ground, arched his back, and became a wolf on four legs.

Then the wolf took the longer path. But he ran on four legs, while the girl walked on two legs, so he reached the cottage before she did.

The wolf bounded through the door and he ate Granny up, every last little bit of her.

Then he stood up on his hind legs and changed from the four-legged furry wolf into the two-legged hairy man. He wriggled into a flowery nightdress and a frilly nightcap, jumped into bed, and pulled the quilt up to his bright yellow eyes.

He waited.

And he waited.

Then the girl pushed open the door. "Granny, it's me! I've brought you a loaf of bread."

"That's lovely, my dear. Bring it here, to the bed."

"Granny," said the girl, "what a deep voice you have!"

"All the better to chat to you with."

The girl stepped closer.

"Granny, what bright eyes you have!"

"All the better to see you with."

She went closer still.

"Granny, what hairy arms you have!"

"All the better to hug you with. Come and sit beside me on the bed."

But the girl stayed where she was.

"I'm not a fool," she said. "I know you're not my granny. You're the man from the path. Where is my granny?"

"She's somewhere warm and cozy, and she left me in charge. So come closer."

The girl didn't want to go any closer. But she didn't think she could run away either. This hairy, toothy man had reached the cottage much faster than her, so if he saw her try to run, he would chase her and catch her.

She must get out of the cottage some other way.

"Come closer," he said again.

"Not yet," she said. "I need to go to the bathroom."

"What?"

"I drank lots at breakfast and now I need to run outside to go to the bathroom."

"No you don't, just come closer."

"I do need to go, I really do." She crossed her legs and jiggled around a bit.

"Come and sit on the bed, girl."

"No. If I sit on the bed, I'll have a little accident. I'll wet the bed, then the quilt will be all damp and stinky. Just let me go out for a minute and I'll come straight back."

"You'll come straight back?"

"Oh yes."

To make sure she did come straight back, the wolf in the bed tied one end of a long string to the girl's ankle and he held the other end in his long fingers.

"Back in a minute . . ." she said, as she shuffled to the door with her legs crossed.

As soon as she stepped outside, instead of going behind a bush and squatting down, she tried to untie the string.

But it was tied very tightly and her fingers were shaking.

The wolf inside the cottage yelled, "Come on, get back in here!"

The girl was struggling to loosen the knot.

"You're taking too long. You can't have drunk *that* much. Come back in here!"

She was pulling so hard on the string

that her nails were breaking and her ankle was bleeding.

"Hurry up, girl!"

She untangled the last knot, pulled the string off, tied the string around a tree, then she ran.

She ran as fast as she could, along the straight path out of the forest.

The wolf in the bed yelled, "Come back in here now!"

She ran as fast as she could, through the shadows of the forest.

The wolf pulled on the string, but the girl didn't come back through the door. The wolf tugged and hauled on the string, and by the time he realized he was trying to pull a tree into the cottage, the girl was halfway home.

He leaped out of bed, ripped off the nightdress and nightcap, and changed back into a wolf on four legs. Then he ran after her.

She raced.

And he chased.

The wolf was much faster on his four legs than the girl was on her two legs, even with

his belly full of granny. But the girl had a head start, she didn't slow down, and she didn't look back. She simply ran and ran and ran.

The wolf was just behind her when she reached the edge of the forest, but she didn't turn around, she didn't falter. She ran right out of the shadow of the trees. She reached her house, she pushed the door open, and she stepped inside.

The wolf reached the edge of the forest.

The girl looked back and saw him. He saw her, just a few steps away.

But he wouldn't leave the forest. And she never went back into the forest.

So that is how the first-ever Little Red Riding Hood escaped the first-ever wolf to wear a nightie, all on her very own, without the help of any hunters or woodcutters.

But there was no happily ever after for her granny, because no one has ever really come out of a wolf's belly alive.

Telesilla and the Gates of Argos

Greek legend

Two and a half thousand years ago, the Spartan army, led by their king, Kleomenes, attacked the city of Argos.

The men of Argos armed themselves and marched out of the city gates to meet the Spartan army, while the city's best-known poet, Telesilla, sang her songs of loyalty and bravery.

The two armies clashed and battled, but the Spartans were the best trained, hardiest, and most vicious warriors in ancient Greece, so they defeated the men of Argos.

Soon, most of the men of Argos lay injured and dying on the land they had tried to defend. The men who were still able to run took shelter in a sacred grove of trees.

The Spartans surrounded the grove, but they were unwilling to go in for fear of angering the gods. So Kleomenes tricked the men of Argos by calling out their names individually and claiming that their families in the city had paid ransoms for their safety. The men came out one by one, and the Spartans killed them one by one.

When the few men left in the grove finally realized they were being tricked and refused to come out, Kleomenes ordered the grove burned down.

Then the Spartans started to march on the city.

The women of Argos, who had watched from the walls, had seen their men defeated

and murdered, and had sung Telesilla's songs of lamentation, now gathered together.

Telesilla said, "We can expect no mercy from these dishonorable Spartans if they enter our city."

One woman said, "We should run."

Another said, "We should bar the gates."

But Telesilla shook her head. "If we run, the Spartans will chase us and catch us. If we bar the gates, the Spartans will break them down, or burn our city like they burned the sacred grove. We must drive the Spartans away."

"How?"

Telesilla explained her plan.

She posted all the children and slaves, all the old men and old women, around the top of the city walls, with pots to look like helmets and brooms to look like javelins.

Then she gathered all the spare armor, shields, helmets, swords, and javelins in the city and armed all the able women.

She led them out of the city and she lined them up to defend the gates of Argos.

There was no time for Telesilla to recite

a stirring poem about courage and honor, because the Spartans were already upon them.

The Spartans ran at the gates, their long spears and short swords still dripping with the blood of the men of Argos, their faces still smeared with ash from the burning sacred grove.

The women of Argos had never trained with weapons. They didn't know how to throw a spear or wield a sword. But they did know how to stand together and how to stand strong. So they stood in a line with Telesilla at their center, their shields overlapping and their blades pointing forward.

And they screamed their defiance.

As the first Spartan blows fell on the women of Argos, and the screams of defiance mixed with screams of pain, Kleomenes shouted: "What voices are those? Are those women's voices? Are we fighting women?" He called on his men to halt.

Then Telesilla pulled off her helmet and said, "We are the women of Argos and we are defending our homes."

Kleomenes frowned. He didn't mind being called a bully or a tyrant or even a cheat. He didn't mind how he won battles against other warriors. But he knew there was no way he could emerge from a battle against women looking strong and glorious.

If he beat them, no one would respect it as a serious victory.

If they beat him, he would be remembered as the king defeated by an army of women.

So he ordered his men to step back and he led them away from the city of Argos.

Telesilla led the women of Argos back through the gates.

As Kleomenes marched his men toward Sparta, he blamed his failure to take Argos on the gods he'd annoyed when he burned the sacred grove.

But the people of Argos knew who had saved them. They put up a marble statue to Telesilla, a statue of a woman with books at her feet and a warrior's helmet in her hand. A statue to celebrate a woman who knew the power of the word and the power of the sword.

Durga and the Demon

Indian myth

Once there was a demon named Mahisha. He was a shape-shifting demon who could take on the shape of any animal but also any shape he invented or desired.

He might choose skin of deep purple or bright pink or pale gray. He might choose scales down his arms, or fur on his back, or feathers on his feet. He might choose claws

on his hands, or tusks on his jaws, or horns on his elbows for jabbing people who got in his way. He might choose black eyeballs or golden teeth. He might choose long barbed tails snaking and flicking around his legs.

But Mahisha wasn't content with his incredible shape-changing powers. He wanted to earn more and greater powers.

So Mahisha denied himself everything for one thousand years. He denied himself food and water, he denied himself light and love and air and warmth. For ten centuries, he denied himself all pleasure and comfort.

This supreme act of denial and determination earned him the right to ask the universe for one more power.

The power he asked for was immortality.

But no one and nothing, not even the universe, can guarantee that you will never die. Mahisha had to ask for something else. So he asked for the next best thing. He asked that he could be killed by no man and no god. And his request was granted.

Armed with that invincibility, the demon set

out to conquer the earth. Because he could not be killed by a man, there was no warrior or general or king or emperor who could defeat him, and soon the demon controlled the whole of the earth.

Then he looked up to heaven. He clawed his way upward, and because he couldn't be killed by a god, he soon conquered heaven too. He grabbed the gods in his huge brightly colored hands and threw them from heaven. He threw Vishnu and Shiva and Brahma and all the rest down to earth.

The gods were homeless and humiliated, and the gods were angry.

They allowed the heat of their anger to burst from their mouths and their bellies. The white hot flames melted together into one bright ball of fury.

And out of that fire stepped . . . a woman.

A tall dark woman named Durga.

Durga was dressed in a bright red sari, and she had ten long, strong, elegant arms.

The gods gave her ten objects to hold in her ten hands:

A thunderbolt

A spear

A bow and arrows

A rope

An ax

A discus

A sword

A trident

A conch shell

And a lotus flower.

Then the gods gave her a tiger to ride on.

Durga rode her tiger up to heaven, where she saw Mahisha, in splendid purple scales, lounging on a golden throne, picking his teeth with a claw, flicking his three tails.

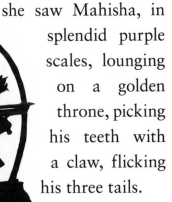

She challenged him by throwing her thunderbolt at his feet.

He laughed. "I can be killed by no man and no god!"

Durga leaped off her tiger and called back, "Do I *look* like a man?"

And she threw her spear at Mahisha's chest.

The sharp point struck him true, driving right through his ribcage. But before his purple body could die, Mahisha changed shape, into a huge lion, which leaped roaring at Durga.

Durga shot the lion in the face with her bow and arrows, and the lion fell whining to the ground. But before the lion's body could die, Mahisha changed into a giant.

He was a giant so tall that his head was above the clouds of heaven. Durga took her rope and threw it around the giant's ankles to trip him up, and as he fell she used her ax to slice open his belly. But before the giant's body could die, Mahisha changed into an elephant.

The elephant wrapped its trunk around the tiger and Durga together, and whirled them around to throw them out of heaven. Durga took her spinning silver discus and sliced off the elephant's trunk. But before the

elephant's body could die, Mahisha changed into a buffalo, which charged heavy-hooved toward Durga.

Durga wrapped all her free hands around the hilt of her sword, swung it, and cut off the buffalo's head.

And fast as fire, before Mahisha could change shape again, Durga leaped on the buffalo's back, wrapped her legs around its ribcage, and squeezed . . .

She squeezed the demon's true form out.

She squeezed a bald, scrawny creature, wrinkled and twisted from his years of denial, out of the bleeding neck of the buffalo.

Durga forced Mahisha's true form out into the light, then she stabbed him through the heart with her trident.

That is how the gods returned home to heaven. That is how people regained control of the earth.

And that is how Mahisha, who couldn't be killed by man or god, was killed by a woman.

Kopecho
and the Two Suns
Venezuelan myth

Once there were two suns in the sky. Two hot, flaming suns, both of them heating and parching the earth. They didn't shine at the same time. They took turns dancing around the earth, so that it was always bright, burning day, never cool, dark night.

It was so hot that plants were dying, rivers were drying, and people were desperate for relief from the heat of the two suns.

So a young girl called Kopecho said that they should get rid of one of the suns. "One sun is enough," she whispered, so the suns up high wouldn't hear her. "Let's get rid of the other one."

"How would we do that?" the rest of the Yupa people whispered back.

"We could drop one sun down a hole deep enough to put out his light forever."

"But who would do that? Who would risk the anger of the suns to trick and attack them?"

Kopecho looked around, hoping someone else would volunteer. But no one did. It was her plan, and they were all staring at her.

She knew that whoever attacked the suns risked death, but also that her people would soon die in this endless burning daylight.

So Kopecho tied her hair back and prepared a feast.

She lit a fire to bake flat bread and to grill the largest fish she could catch in the shallow river, then she picked the juiciest fruit she could find in the shrinking forest.

She dug a pit, so deep and dark that even the suns up high couldn't see its bottom, if they bothered to look. But Kopecho had asked all of her people to dig that day, and hundreds of people were digging ditches, toilets, graves, and foundations for huts, so that if the suns looked down they wouldn't notice one young girl digging a deep pit.

When she had dug as far down as she could, when her tools struck stone rather than earth, she climbed out of the pit, and covered it with thin sticks and broad leaves. Then she let her hair out and called the suns down to a feast.

"Look what I have cooked for you, suns. I admire your heat and light, and your dance in the sky, so I have made you a feast."

The suns came down to earth, to join her in the feast.

She fed them. She sang to them. She flattered them.

Then she said, shyly, hiding her mouth behind her long black hair, "I love to watch you both dance in the sky. Would you please dance with me?"

She stood up and whirled around, her long black hair spreading out like sun's rays. She turned and twirled, she jumped and spun.

The suns laughed and they both got up to dance with her.

The suns liked to dance in curves and circles because they were used to dancing across the sky, but now the girl danced in a straight line, backing toward the pit, leading the suns along with her.

Kopecho realized that she couldn't let both the suns fall in the pit, because no day would be as bad as no night. So she grasped the hand of one sun and though his heat burned her fingers, she smiled as she spun him away from the pit. Then she grasped the hand of the other sun, and she laughed as she spun him *toward* the pit.

She leaped backward, right over the pit, pulling the sun with her, and he landed heavily on the leaves and sticks.

The sticks broke, the leaves fluttered down.

And the sun dropped into the pit.

The sun screamed as he fell.

The other sun stopped dancing. The girl stood on the edge of the pit. They watched the sun's light flicker as he fell down the deep dark hole.

Then the sun hit the hard stone at the bottom and his light faded.

But his light didn't go out completely.

The fall didn't kill the sun, it just injured him. The fall didn't put out his heat and his light, it just cooled the heat and dimmed the light.

So he hauled himself out of the pit, crawled back into the sky, and tried to shine again. But he didn't shine as bright, he shined colder and bluer and less often.

He became the moon.

He still danced with his brother, sun and moon circling in the sky.

And the people were happy. They had a sun in daytime and a moon at night, and just enough light and heat, balanced by enough dark and cold, to live and grow and thrive.

But the moon and his brother the sun were furious with Kopecho, who had tricked

them with food and dance, and had broken their power.

So one early morning when the sun was rising and the moon was still visible, they linked their rays, they picked Kopecho up, and they threw her into the river to drown.

But as she tumbled through the air, Kopecho turned into a frog, and was able to live healthy and happy in the river.

Then, over the years, because of her wisdom, her courage, and her knowledge of the depths from digging down so deep, Kopecho became the Yupa goddess of the underworld, safe and hidden forever from both the sun and the moon.

Mbango
and the Whirlpool
Cameroonian Folktale

Mbango's mother died when she was a baby, so she was brought up by her mother's sister. Her aunt had a daughter of her own, the same age as Mbango, but the aunt didn't treat the two girls equally.

She gave her own daughter all the best food and let her lie around in the sun. She fed Mbango the leftovers and made her do the

hardest, nastiest, dirtiest jobs around their hut. If she wasn't satisfied with the work Mbango did, she beat her with a stick.

Mbango's first job every morning was to go to the river to fill the family's calabash with water for cooking and drinking.

One day, Mbango slipped on the mud of the riverbank and dropped the calabash into the water.

The river swept the calabash away. Mbango knew her aunt would beat her if she went home without their only calabash, so she chased it, running along the riverbank, keeping pace with the calabash as the current pulled it along, hoping it would get tangled in weeds or come close enough to the bank for her to reach it.

But it was swept onward, far out in the speeding river, until Mbango saw a whirlpool ahead. The water was swirling so fast that the center of the whirlpool was a sharp hole in the river.

The calabash started to spin, sweeping in circles around the edge of the whirlpool, then being pulled nearer the center. Mbango

 53

watched as the calabash was dragged toward the middle, then vanished down the hole and into the depths of the river.

She was more scared of telling her aunt that she had lost their only calabash than she was of the whirlpool. So she closed her eyes, clasped her hands over her head, and dove in.

She dove right down to the riverbed, and when she opened her eyes, she found that she was standing in a village of huts just like her own. She was standing upright, she wasn't wet, and she could breathe. But when she looked up, instead of the sky, she saw the whirlpool spinning above her.

When she looked back down, she saw the calabash. It had landed on the riverbed, and a little old lady had just picked it up.

The little old lady was bent and hunched, with a wrinkled face, bright black eyes, and a wide grin showing how few teeth she had left. She was stroking the calabash.

Mbango said to the old lady, "I'm sorry, but that's my calabash and I dove down here to fetch it."

"That's a shame," said the little old lady. "I don't have a calabash and this is a lovely one."

Mbango said, "I am truly sorry, but I do have to take it back to my own village, because if I go home without it, my aunt will beat me. Why don't I offer you a fair exchange? I'll do a day's work for you, then you can give me the calabash back."

So the little old lady took Mbango to her home, a rickety hut at the edge of the village, with a couple of pigs snuffling outside. Mbango spent all day doing the jobs the little old lady was too hunched and weak to do. She fixed the roof and patched the walls, she cleaned the pig pens, and cleaned the hut inside and out.

When her hut was neat and tidy, the little old lady said, "I think it's time you went back to your own world and took this calabash to your aunt."

Mbango sighed and nodded.

"But before you go, I'd be very happy if you'd share a meal with me," said the little old lady.

So Mbango sat down at the little old lady's table.

Then, with her face shining, her eyes bright and her wide mouth grinning, the little old lady put a plate in front of Mbango. "Please eat. I hardly ever have guests, and I'd be so honored if you'd eat with me."

Mbango looked down.

At a plate of PIG DUNG.

She looked up at the little old lady's eager face and bright eyes.

She looked back down at the plate of pig dung.

Mbango thought, "I don't want to be rude, I don't want to disappoint or insult this nice old lady, but this is *pig dung.* I can't eat pig dung."

She looked at the little old lady's happy face and she thought, "I've done things that are almost as horrid for my aunt and I don't even like her. But I do like this nice old lady and I don't want to offend her."

So she put her hand out, she picked up the smallest piece of pig dung, and she lifted it to her lips . . .

As she put it to her mouth, it turned into a handful of ndole, her favorite fish stew.

Mbango ate everything on the plate and each piece of pig dung turned into wonderful, tasty food.

"This is the best meal I've ever had," she said to the little old lady, who bounced up and down with happiness.

Then the little old lady gave Mbango the calabash and said, "I have an extra gift for you too, to say thank you for being so helpful and so kind." She held out three large eggs. "Break these eggs on the floor of the hut when you get home and they might change your life."

Mbango said, "Thank you," then jumped out of the village, swam up toward the whirlpool, scrambled onto the riverbank, and ran home to her aunt's hut.

Her aunt picked up a stick and waved it at Mbango. "Where have you been, you lazy, inconsiderate child?"

Mbango explained, "I dropped the calabash in the river, then I chased it until it vanished

into a whirlpool, so I dove in to get it back. And I found a village under the river, and met a little old lady who gave me back the calabash and these three eggs, and told me to break the eggs on the floor."

She broke the first egg and out slithered silver chains.

She broke the second egg and out dropped gold nuggets.

She broke the third egg and out tumbled handfuls of diamonds.

The aunt stared at the riches on the floor, then she prodded her own daughter with the stick. "Go and get us three of those eggs, girl. Go on, now."

So Mbango's cousin grabbed the calabash and ran to the river. She threw the calabash into the water, she ran along the bank, she saw it vanish into the whirlpool, then she held her nose and jumped in after it.

She found herself in the village, with the whirlpool spinning above. She saw the little old lady stroking the calabash and she yelled, "Oi! Give that back, it's mine!"

The little old lady handed her the calabash and said, "Before you go, I'd be honored if you would join me for a meal."

"I suppose I'd better," said Mbango's cousin.

So the little old lady sat her down and offered her a plate of . . .

"PIG DUNG! You want me to eat pig dung? That's disgusting, you horrible, weird old woman. I'm not eating that!" The cousin stood up, knocking over the table and the plate. "Just give me my three eggs and I'll be off."

The little old lady stared at her for a moment, then handed her three eggs. "I hope you enjoy them."

Mbango's cousin left the village, swam out of the whirlpool, clambered out of the river, ran home, and shouted, "I got three eggs!"

She smashed the first egg and out slithered snakes.

She threw the second egg against the wall, where it shattered and out dropped scorpions.

She screamed and let go of the third

egg, which cracked on the floor and out tumbled spiders.

The snakes and scorpions and spiders chased the aunt and the cousin into the forest. They were never seen again, and that made Mbango's life much happier than any of her new riches—although she enjoyed the riches too!

Hervor and the Cursed Sword

Norse legend

This is a story of a sword called Tyrfing. The sword was created when a man named Sigrlami snuck up on two dwarves one night and blocked their way back to the safety of their cave. He threatened to keep them trapped on the surface of the earth until the sun came up and turned them to stone, unless they agreed to forge a perfect sword for him.

The dwarves made Sigrlami a beautiful sword, but as they gave him the sword, they put a curse on it, saying that every time Tyrfing was drawn from its sheath, it must be sheathed in blood before it could be put back.

But Sigrlami was a warrior and he didn't think that was a curse.

So his sword Tyrfing brought him great wealth and fame, because every time it was drawn, it had to spill blood.

He passed Tyrfing on to his first-born son, who won fame, then passed Tyrfing on to his first-born son, who won fame, then passed Tyrfing on to *his* first-born son ... As the sword was passed down from father to son, the curse got stronger and stronger, and the sword spilled more and more blood.

Until the last of the line of first-born sons, Angantyr, carried Tyrfing into battle with his eleven brothers by his side, and much blood was spilled, including the life blood of all twelve brothers.

Because the sword was cursed, and because Angantyr had no sons, the sword was buried

with him. The twelve brothers and their swords were all buried together on a small island.

Angantyr had no sons, but he did have a daughter. Hervor was a baby when her father and uncles died. As she grew up, she didn't want to learn embroidery or baking or fancy ways to braid her hair. She wrestled with the local boys and learned to fight with wooden sticks. She wanted to be a warrior and a pirate, battling and raiding, winning fame and fortune.

So when Hervor was grown, she announced that she would be a Viking, like her father and uncles, like her grandfather and great-grandfather. She announced that she would lead a shipload of warriors, she would raid the sea and the coasts, and she would bring gold and fame back home.

But no one followed her. Why would they? She was a girl and she was unproven.

Hervor needed to prove herself. She needed to show who she was and who she could be. She needed Tyrfing, her father's famous sword.

So she paid a boatman to take her to the

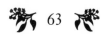

island where her father's body was buried. As they rowed nearer the island's shore, the boatman said, "It's almost dusk. The locals say the island is haunted at night. I'm not rowing any closer, and if you take my advice, girl, you won't go ashore either."

Hervor shrugged. "If it's haunted, it's haunted by my family."

She leaped into the water and swam ashore.

Then she started to walk to the middle of the small island. Though it was a clear night on the water, the island was covered in fog. Knee-high fog, clammy and clinging, heavy and hard to push aside. Hervor waded through the fog and with every step she took, the fog moaned and groaned and howled around her legs.

She saw a high mound of earth ahead. It was the grave of her father and uncles. As she reached the mound, the earth burst into flames. She sprinted through the fire, her wet dress hissing around her.

She reached the top of the mound, balanced on the crumbling edge of a black

pit, then jumped down and landed hard on dusty ground.

She stood up, surrounded by a circle of twelve tall pale men, each bloodied with wounds, all staring at her.

They whispered insults at her for waking them and took slow dragging steps toward her.

Hervor looked calmly around the circle. All the men had swords, but only one sword was glowing: the top of the blade of a gold-handled, tightly sheathed sword glowed brightly in the hands of the tallest, bloodiest man.

"Father," she called out. "Angantyr. Father. I am your daughter Hervor and I have come to claim my sword."

The men stopped moving, but kept staring at her.

The man with the glowing sword shook his head, and his head creaked and wobbled on his shoulders. "But you are a girl. You cannot have this sword, you are not strong enough or brave enough to carry a sword with a blood curse."

Hervor laughed. "I have swum ashore to a haunted island. I have waded through

howling fog and run through grave-mound flames. I have leaped into a death pit and faced twelve bloodied ghosts. Am I not brave and strong, Father?"

Her father simply said, "If you think you want Tyrfing, then come and take it."

Hervor stepped forward and jerked the sword out of his cold grip. "I have the sword now, I carry the responsibility of the blood curse. Now you can all lie down and go back to your long sleep."

The men laid down, and Hervor hauled herself out of the grave, walked through the cool, clear night to the shore, then swam out to the boat waiting a safe distance away.

Hervor told the story of the grave and the sword to all who would listen, and men knew that the sword's curse gave it power, so they followed her willingly. Hervor gathered a shipload of Vikings, she fought in many famous battles, and led many successful raids. And her sword was never drawn from its sheath without being sheathed in blood. But Hervor didn't think that was a curse, because with

Tyrfing in her hand Hervor spilled the blood
of enough men to became rich and respected.

When Hervor grew old she gave Tyrfing to
her sons. What happened to them is another
story, but it's not a peaceful or cheerful one,
because the dwarf-made sword still carried
its curse . . .

Visiting Baba Yaga

Russian Folktale

Once upon a time a little girl lived happily with her father in a cottage on the edge of the forest. But when her father remarried and a new stepmother arrived, the little girl became less happy and more scared.

In real life stepmothers are usually lovely, but this little girl had a good reason to be afraid of her stepmother.

Her stepmother was the sister of Baba Yaga,

and Baba Yaga was the most famous, the most feared, the most ferocious witch in the whole Russian forest.

Baba Yaga had iron teeth, sharp and glittering and strong.

Baba Yaga lived in a hut built on a pair of hen's legs, always bending and shifting and scratching the ground.

Baba Yaga traveled in a mortar and pestle, sitting in the giant bowl and using the long pestle to bounce herself along the ground.

And Baba Yaga ate children for supper.

So the little girl was afraid of her stepmother, because she thought that her stepmother would try to feed her to Baba Yaga.

The little girl was right.

One day, the stepmother said, "I want to do some sewing. Fetch me some pins from my sister in the forest."

The little girl broke the back off the brooch which held her red shawl together and gave the metal spike to her stepmother. "You can use this as a pin, so I don't need to go into the forest."

The stepmother sniffed. "I still need thread.

Fetch me some thread from my sister in the forest."

The little girl found a loose thread on the fringe of her shawl, pulled it out carefully, and gave the red thread to her stepmother. "You can sew with this, so I don't need to go into the forest."

The stepmother sniffed, then smiled. She bent the pin and dropped the thread on the fire. "Now do as I say. Fetch me pins and thread from my sister in the forest."

The little girl sighed. She couldn't keep finding ways to avoid Baba Yaga, she had to go and face her. So the little girl combed her hair out of her eyes with her polished wooden comb and put a slice of sausage and a slice of bread in a blue napkin, then walked into the forest.

She walked along the gray gritty path, comb in her hair and picnic in her hand, until she stubbed her toe on a smooth white pebble. She looked at the pebble on the gray path, then looked around. There were no other white pebbles and no white rocks nearby. She smiled.

"You look out of place in this forest, just like me." She put the pebble in her pocket.

She kept walking through the forest, comb in her hair, picnic in her hand, pebble in her pocket.

After a long hungry walk, the little girl saw a wooden hut on two scaly orange legs. She had reached Baba Yaga's house.

The little girl clambered up and tried to get in the door. But a dog barked and growled at her. She could see the sharpness of the dog's ribs though its mangy hair, so she gave the dog the slice of bread. The dog let her pass into the house.

Then a cat leaped at her, hissing and spitting. She could see the knobbles of the cat's spine through its flea-bitten fur, so she gave the slice of sausage to the cat. The cat purred and left her alone.

Then a young woman in ragged clothes, shivering and blowing her nose, stepped out of the shadows. "Why have you come to my mother's house? We don't often get willing visitors." The young woman sneezed and

coughed. The little girl pulled off her warm, red shawl and wrapped it around the young woman's shoulders.

Then a loud voice boomed from the weaving loom in the corner. "Get out of the way, daughter, so I can see what my sister has sent me!"

Baba Yaga stamped toward the little girl, her wide smile showing all her polished iron teeth.

The little girl said, "I've come to fetch pins and thread, please."

"My dear child, I have plenty of pins and thread, there on the shelf by the loom. And you may have them before you go. But first . . ."

Baba Yaga leaned over the little girl, prodding her and sniffing her. "But first, after your long journey, let's give you a nice hot bath.

"Daughter, fill that pot by the fire. Girl, sit on my stool and weave, so I'll hear the shuttle and know you're still here. Cat, watch the girl. Dog, guard the

door. I'll fetch some herbs and spices for the water, to make you taste . . . er . . . smell nice."

Baba Yaga stepped into the pantry to look for herbs and spices.

The little girl started to weave. *Click clack, click clack.*

The daughter, in her red shawl, started to fill the pot. But she was using a sieve to carry the water.

The cat watched the shuttle, washing the grease off her whiskers.

The dog sat in the doorway, crumbs on his nose.

And Baba Yaga yelled from inside the pantry, "Are you still there, girl?"

"Yes." The little girl kept weaving. *Click clack, click clack.*

Baba Yaga yelled, "Is the bath full yet, daughter?" The daughter said, "Not yet," as she carried another dripping sieve over.

Then the cat jumped up on the stool, put her paw on the shuttle, and began pushing it. The little girl stood up and grabbed pins and thread from the shelf, then she smiled at

the daughter and stepped over the dog, who wagged his tail.

The little girl started to run home.

Baba Yaga heard the shuttle click clack, click clack and she didn't hear the dog bark, so she stayed in the pantry searching for herbs and spices.

The little girl ran and ran as fast as she could, through the forest toward her home.

Then Baba Yaga found the dill, horseradish, and caraway seeds, so she stepped back into the room.

She saw the cat sitting on the stool making a terrible tangle with the wool, the dog wagging his tail at the empty doorway, and her daughter carrying a wet sieve to the pot.

Baba Yaga screamed, "How *dare* you all betray me? Why would you betray your own Baba Yaga?"

The cat said, "All the time I've lived here, you've fed me nothing but dead mice. That little girl gave me sausage."

The dog said, "All the time I've lived here, you've fed me nothing but dry bones. That

little girl gave me fresh bread."

The daughter said, "All the time I've lived here, you've given me nothing but rags to wear. That little girl gave me a warm, red shawl."

Baba Yaga gnashed her iron teeth and screeched, "I'll be back to deal with you all, once I've caught my supper!"

She leaped into her mortar and thumped her pestle on the ground.

The little girl heard the thumping and ran faster.

But the thumping got louder and closer. The little girl knew that Baba Yaga would soon catch up with her, so she pulled the polished wooden comb from her hair and threw it behind her.

As soon as the comb hit the ground, it turned into a tight-packed, thorny hedge. Baba Yaga couldn't fit her mortar and pestle between the thorns, so she had to stop chasing.

The little girl ran.

Baba Yaga used her iron teeth to cut down the hedge and started chasing the little girl again.

The little girl heard the thumping get louder and closer, so she threw the blue napkin behind her.

As soon as the napkin hit the ground, it turned into a deep blue lake. Baba Yaga couldn't thump her pestle on the water, so she had to stop chasing.

The little girl ran.

Baba Yaga bent down, drank up all the lake, and started chasing the little girl again.

The little girl heard the thumping get louder and closer, so she found the white pebble in her pocket and threw it behind her.

As soon as the pebble hit the ground it turned into a high, icy mountain range.

Baba Yaga started to climb the mountains, but before she reached the top, she was frozen solid by the cold. She stuck to the mountain, with icicles dangling from her iron teeth. And the last anyone heard, she was still there.

So the little girl went home, and when the stepmother saw her step-daughter return safely from Baba Yaga's hut carrying pins and thread, she was so afraid of the little girl's

cleverness and power that she ran away and was never seen again.

Baba Yaga's dog and cat and daughter lived happily in the hut on hen's legs. And they always ate sausage and bread for supper. Never ever little girls.

Aliquipiso and the Cliffs

American Indian legend

Long ago, the Oneida were a small cultural group and their age-old enemies the Mingos were a much larger group, with many more warriors.

One year, the Mingos attacked in force. This time they didn't just want to win a few minor battles with the Oneida. This time they

wanted to destroy them. The Mingos drove the Oneida from their villages, killed most of the men, and captured many of the women and children.

The survivors found a hiding place in the high rocks and cliffs of the mountains, following secret paths known only to their people, but they knew they were not safe forever.

"The Mingos are still searching and will find our trail eventually," the elders said, as they sat in council. "And our food is running out, so we may starve before they find us."

"We don't need to wait here to die," said a young girl called Aliquipiso. "I have an idea. We are sheltering at the top of a high cliff, we are surrounded by sharp and heavy rocks. If we can get the Mingo warriors to gather at the foot of the cliff, we can throw the rocks down and crush them. If they lose their warriors, they will go home and leave us in peace."

"But how can we get them all to stand in the right place, just where we can aim rocks at them?" asked the elders.

"I will go down and lure the warriors to the

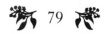

perfect spot, then I will shout when it is time for you to throw the rocks."

"But Aliquipiso, if you lure them into position and you shout for the rocks, then you will be crushed too."

"I know. But I would rather die down there taking my enemies with me, than wait for death up here, watching my people dying around me."

The elders praised Aliquipiso's wisdom and blessed her courage, they hung precious shell necklaces around her neck, and they promised she would never be forgotten.

Then Aliquipiso said good-bye and she crept down the secret path from the cliffs to the land below.

As she wandered toward the smoldering remains of her village, looking lost and confused, she was spotted by Mingo scouts, who captured her and took her to their chief.

"Do you know where your people are hiding, girl?" he yelled at her.

"I will never tell you," said Aliquipiso.

"So you do know! And you will tell me."

"No, I will never betray my people," she said.

"Yes, you will, if you want to live."

The Mingo chief leaned over to whisper threats and promises in her ear, until Aliquipiso sobbed and begged for mercy. "Please don't hurt me! If you don't hurt me, I'll show you the secret path to the hiding place."

They laughed at her weakness and her cowardice, and they let her lead them, the whole warrior band, to the foot of the cliffs.

Aliquipiso put her finger to her lips and signaled them to be quiet. She whispered, "Come close and I will tell you the secrets of my people and show you the hidden path to our sanctuary."

The warriors drew closer to the girl.

She whispered more softly and beckoned them closer.

They crowded in nearer and nearer to hear her.

When the Mingo warriors were all gathered around her, in a tight, close circle, Aliquipiso shouted "Now!"

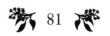

The Oneida threw hundreds of heavy sharp rocks down on the heads of their enemies and crushed them.

The rocks also crushed the girl who had led her enemies into the trap.

The rocks killed Aliquipiso.

But her plan worked. The Mingo people were so weakened by the loss of their young men that they left the Oneida in peace.

The Oneida went home and rebuilt their villages, and the group grew and prospered.

And because the elders had blessed Aliquipiso's cleverness and courage, and her people had promised she would never be forgotten, Aliquipiso became part of the land: her long hair became the tendrils of

the woodbine and her red blood became the flowers of the honeysuckle.

The Oneida still tell the story of the girl who saved their people, grandparents passing on the story to children around the campfire. Aliquipiso's story will be passed on with pride and gratitude for as long as there are Oneida on this earth, and as long as woodbine and honeysuckle grow out of this earth.

Tokoyo
and the Skin Rope

Japanese legend

Tokoyo lived long ago in a village on the coast of Japan. Her father was a healer who believed that he should never walk past someone who needed his skills, that if someone was injured or ill, he should always stop to help. He hoped to teach Tokoyo how to be a healer too, he hoped to share his skills and his knowledge of herbs with her.

But Tokoyo had a different passion. She loved to dive with the pearl fishers of the coast, the women who trained long and hard to dive deep under the waves. Tokoyo was learning to how to hold her breath for minutes at a time, to search for oysters, then pry them open with a knife to see if there was a pearl inside.

Tokoyo loved the challenge of holding her breath, she loved the underwater world where light and sound were so different from onshore, and she loved the gamble of not knowing which oysters would contain pearls.

One day the local warlord fell ill. Tokoyo's father tried to heal him, but it was an illness the healer had never seen before. The warlord was struggling to breathe, his lungs were filling up with fluid, he felt like he was very slowly drowning. Tokoyo's father, even with all his learning, skills and herbs, couldn't heal the warlord. So the warlord, who couldn't tolerate failure, exiled Tokoyo's father.

Her father was sent to a far-away island to be imprisoned, never to come home again. He

was exiled so fast that Tokoyo didn't even get a chance to say goodbye.

She decided to follow him to the island, to find him, to keep him company, perhaps even to help him escape.

After a long journey she arrived on the island and started to search. The island was very different from her own coastal home. No one dove for pearls; instead the men fished with long nets, from small boats.

As she searched the shore for any signs of her father's prison, she saw something glitter in the morning sun. She saw a silver shape on a high rock above a stony beach.

She ran closer. It was a girl, in a silver robe, being pushed to the edge of the rock by a priest. The girl was screaming and struggling.

Tokoyo shouted, "No!" and ran toward the rock.

She ran past a line of men on the beach, local fishermen in a half-circle around the rock, who weren't doing anything to help the girl.

"No!" Tokoyo shouted again and scrambled up the rock.

She stood between the girl and the edge, holding her arms out to block the way. "What are you doing?" she asked the priest.

"I'm throwing her into the sea."

"Why? Can she even swim?" Tokoyo glanced at the girl, who shook her head. "Why would you throw a girl who can't swim into the sea? She'll die!"

The priest nodded. "Someone must die, because there is a giant sea serpent living under this island, and he causes storms which sink our boats and drown our fishermen unless we give him a gift once a year. A gift of a girl, to eat. So if we don't throw this girl into the sea, then our fishermen will die."

Tokoyo looked at the weeping girl and at the frightened faces of the fishermen below. She thought of her father, who never walked past someone who needed his help. She took a slow breath, deep into her strong lungs. She felt the breath fill her body and she knew how long she could hold it. She felt the sharp oyster knife in the waistband of her dark tunic.

Tokoyo said, "If you must give the giant serpent a gift, then give me."

"You?" said the priest. "You would sacrifice yourself for this girl?"

"Yes, but will you do me one favor in return? There is a healer imprisoned on this island. Please take him a message from me. Tell him that his daughter came looking for him, but that I stopped to help someone on the way."

Then Tokoyo balanced on the edge of the rock above the sea and stretched her arms upward.

"Not yet," called the priest. "You must wear the silver robe, so the sea serpent knows you are the gift and leaves our boats alone."

The girl undid the silver belt and pulled off the silver robe, and Tokoyo tied it around herself.

She stood on the edge again, her arms raised. The priest stepped toward her, but she shook her head. "There is no need to push me. I go willingly." She took a deep breath and dove off the rock.

She dove down down down, into the flat, cold sea.

Tokoyo could see underwater, but not clearly, because light moves differently under the sea, as if the light from above and the shadows from below ripple together. However she could see enough to glimpse a black arch in the bottom of the rock. A cave. The cave where the giant sea serpent lived.

To one side of the cave, Tokoyo saw a man, standing on the seabed. She swam closer.

The man was just standing, staring at her. Eyes wide open, mouth wide open.

She swam even closer. Was the sea monster a man, rather than a serpent?

She swam cautiously closer still, then she recognized the man. He was the warlord who had exiled her father.

She swam closer and the man just stared, he didn't move. This wasn't a man, this was a statue. A wooden statue of the warlord, deep underwater.

She looked at the statue's wide open mouth, full of seawater, and she thought about the

illness her father couldn't cure, and she wondered . . .

Suddenly there was a surge of water from the dark arch, which knocked Tokoyo over. She tumbled through the sea.

When she regained control, she was already in the serpent's mouth. Huge fangs above her and huge fangs below her were closing around her. So she put her feet against the forked tongue coiled at the back of the mouth, and she kicked, pushing herself off and propelling herself fast through the water and out of the serpent's mouth.

The mouth snapped shut and Tokoyo saw the sea serpent, huge and yellow and scaly, look confused at the lack of food in its mouth.

She turned and swam off, zigging and zagging, trying to get away from that giant yellow head. But the sea serpent followed her, weaving and winding through the water.

Tokoyo was fast and tricky, but the sea serpent was faster and followed her every move. Then with a lurch and a snap, the

serpent had her. The hem of her silver robe was trapped between the monster's fangs. She couldn't get away, she was dangling from the serpent's mouth, looking up into its huge hungry eyes.

Tokoyo jerked and tugged on the silver fabric, trying to escape, but she couldn't tear herself free. She fumbled under the robe and pulled out her oyster knife.

With one slash she cut off the hem and freed herself.

The serpent's mouth opened in surprise, the fabric which Tokoyo had cut away slid out from between the fangs, and Tokoyo saw the sea serpent's eyes flick to watch the silver ribbon drift away.

She realized that the sea serpent was chasing the silver robe, not her. The silver was bright in the dim, rippling water, so the wrapping around the gift was what allowed the serpent to catch its food.

She undid the silver belt and pulled off the silver robe. Then she threw the robe in one direction and she dove, in her dark tunic, in

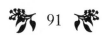

the other direction. The sea serpent snapped after the robe, not after the dark shadow.

As the sea serpent's head turned away from her, Tokoyo dove toward it and stabbed the serpent's right eye. She jerked out the knife and the sea serpent's black blood darkened the sea. She swam over the sea serpent's head, stabbed the left eye, and tugged her knife free again. Then she dove under the sea serpent's jaws and cut right across its throat.

But she didn't take out the knife a third time.

Tokoyo left the knife in the sea serpent's flesh and dove down and around its long writhing body. She swam in a spiral around the serpent, cutting all the way, slicing off a long line of yellow skin as she dove.

As she swam around and down, the blood spurted from the serpent's flesh, but as she cut more and more, the flow of blood slowed, until it was only seeping out.

When she reached the tail of the serpent with her sharp knife, the blood stopped completely and she knew the monster was dead.

She used her knife to cut the strip of skin off at the tail and the sea serpent drifted to the seabed, naked and skinless and dead.

Tokoyo held in her hand a long strong scaly yellow skin rope.

She could feel her lungs straining. Her body needed air. But she swam to the statue and tied the skin rope around its waist. Then holding the other end, she swam upward, not rushing, taking her time, staying safe all the way up to the surface.

Her face burst up into the air. She took a deep and welcome breath.

Then she swam to the shore. She put the skin rope in the hands of the girl she had saved, the priest she had persuaded, and the long curve of fishermen, and she asked them to pull. They hauled and dragged that wooden statue out of the water.

When it was on the shore, Tokoyo turned it over to let the water drain out.

When the statue's mouth was empty and the wood started to dry, the warlord in her village far away breathed properly again.

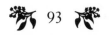

When he discovered that Tokoyo had lifted the curse on him, he let Tokoyo and her father return to their village, where her father healed anyone who needed his help and Tokoyo dove for pearls.

But whenever she went to that beautiful and dangerous underwater world, she took a silver sash tucked into her dark tunic, in case she ever needed to distract another giant sea serpent.

The Giant's Heart
Scottish Folktale

O nce there was a boy who left home with nothing but his sword, to seek his fortune.

He walked into the forest and the first thing he saw was a wolf with its paw caught in a steel trap. The boy pried the trap open with his sword and the wolf said, "Thank you for freeing me. If you ever need my help, just call me."

The boy walked on and saw a hawk with its feet caught in birdlime on a post. The boy eased the hawk's talons loose and the hawk said, "Thank you for freeing me. If you ever need my help, just call me."

The boy walked on, thinking that he wasn't making his fortune, but at least he was making friends.

By the river, he saw an otter tangled in a fishing net. He cut the net open with his sword and the otter said, "Thank you for freeing me. If you ever need my help, just call me."

The boy walked on, deeper and deeper into the forest, until he heard a scream ahead of him. He ran to the edge of a clearing in the trees, where he saw a girl with a charred rope around her waist being dragged through the grass by a huge giant.

"Let me go!" the girl screamed.

"No!" boomed the giant. "I will not let you escape again. I will chain you up if you keep burning through my ropes. And I won't let you go until your father stops sending heroes to kill me and starts sending gold to ransom you!"

As he wrapped a chain around the girl's waist and shoved her into a dark cave, the giant said, "If I don't get money soon, I'm going to eat you, just like I've eaten all those boys with their swords."

On the edge of the clearing, the boy with the sword shivered. But he couldn't leave a human being in a trap when he had rescued a wolf, a hawk, and an otter, so he waited until night fell, then he crept up to the cave entrance. He crouched down by an old tree stump and listened. He heard monstrously loud snoring, which he hoped was the giant, and he crept in.

In the light of the fire flickering in the center of the cave, he saw rugs and stools, barrels and pots, shelves and cupboards. He saw the girl curled up under a thin lace shawl by one side of the fire, and on the other side, the giant sleeping under a velvet quilt, with an ax by his huge hand.

The boy tiptoed up to the giant. He lifted his sword high and slashed down hard. The giant's head rolled off his neck, and the boy said, "*Yes!*"

Then he ran to the girl. "I have saved you!"

"No you haven't. Hide yourself. Now!"

"But . . ."

"Don't argue. Don't be like the others. Don't waste time arguing. Just *hide*!"

So the boy hid behind a big barrel.

And he saw the giant sit up, pick up his head and put it back on his neck with a squelchy, grinding sound.

Then the giant stood up and grabbed his ax. "Who did that? Where is he? I'll roast him for my breakfast."

"No, you won't," said the girl calmly. "He ran off. He didn't wait around like the others for you to eat him. He'll be long gone now. Just go back to sleep."

So the giant lay down and once he was snoring again, the girl lifted her chain quietly and came around behind the barrel.

"Thanks for trying to save me," she whispered to the boy. "But this giant can't be killed with a sword."

"Why not? I cut off his head. That's usually a killing blow."

"He can't be killed that easily because his heart isn't in his body. It's hidden in a safe place, so his body can't die."

"Where is his heart then?" the boy asked.

"Well, he says it's in that cupboard there . . ."

So the boy got up, climbed the cave wall, opened the cupboard quietly, and looked inside.

It was empty.

He climbed down and tiptoed back to the girl.

"It's empty."

"Of course it's empty. I've been here for weeks, I've already looked. Anyway, he's not foolish enough to tell me where it really is when I just ask him a straight question. But if you would like to help me, perhaps we can find his heart together. Could you stay hidden here, and just watch and listen?"

The boy nodded, then spent an uncomfortable night and morning crunched up between the barrel and the cave wall. First he watched the giant sleep, then wake, then have his breakfast. Then he watched the giant go out hunting, leaving the girl on a long chain

so she could cook and clean and shake the rugs and work on quilting at the entrance to the cave.

The boy stood up and stretched. "Why don't I break your chain with my sword right now, rather than waiting for a chance to find the giant's heart?"

She smiled. "No, he never goes very far away, so if we make too much clattering and clanging trying to break the chain, he'll hear us and rush back. Please hide again, and let me find the heart my own way."

Then the girl stood on a giant-sized stool and polished the cupboard door. The boy watched as she hung garlands of flowers around it, painted little love hearts on it, and tied her own hair ribbon around the handle.

When the giant came back in the evening, the boy watched and listened as the giant pointed to the cupboard and said, "What's all that?"

"I just wanted to make the cupboard pretty," said the girl, "because you said it was where you kept your heart."

"Why would you do that?"

The girl looked a bit embarrassed, and muttered, "Because in the weeks I've been here, dear giant, I've grown fond of you. And I wanted to show you how my heart felt, by decorating *your* heart's home."

The giant sniggered. "You silly little girl. I'm holding you hostage! I'm going to *eat* you if your father doesn't fill my cave with gold. Why would you try to decorate my heart's home? You foolish little girl!"

The girl blushed. "Well, I know you're a nasty big giant, but I'm lonely here and I feel like you're my only friend."

The giant laughed out loud, showing all his crooked, brown teeth. "I'm not your friend! And I'm not impressed by flowers and ribbons. Anyway, that's not even where my heart is, you silly little girl!"

"Isn't it? So I've decorated the wrong place!" She sniffled. "Oh dear. Because I thought if I decorated your heart's home, you might like me even just a little bit more . . ."

"Ha! I'm not that stupid! Anyway, you can't

decorate my heart's true home, because that chain I've got around your waist won't reach as far as the tree stump outside the cave! And even if you could decorate the tree stump with ridiculous ribbons and wimpy flowers, you couldn't reach inside the stump to decorate the deer, or the duck inside the deer, or the salmon inside the duck, or the egg inside the salmon, which is where my heart really is. So give up, girl. I don't want ribbons and flowers. I want gold. And if I don't get gold, I'm going to eat you up, whether you simper and smile at me or not."

The giant laughed again and ripped the ribbon off the cupboard door. The girl sat down and sobbed. But the boy sat behind the barrel and smiled. Now he knew what he had to do the next day.

The boy and the girl waited all night, listening to the giant's snores, then once the giant left the cave, the boy stood up and stretched and joined the girl at the cave entrance.

The chain around her waist wouldn't allow the girl to reach the tree stump, but the boy

took three steps forward, lifted his sword, and sliced open the tree stump.

A sleek deer leaped out and started to run off. The boy called "Wolf!" and the wolf he had freed sprinted out of the forest and chased the deer.

When the wolf brought the deer down, a shining duck flew out of the deer's mouth and flapped off into the air. The boy called "Hawk!" and the hawk swooped down out of the sky and grasped the duck in its talons.

A silver salmon fell out of the duck's beak, landed in the river and swam away. The boy called "Otter!" and the otter slid into the water and chased the salmon. When the otter dragged the salmon out of the river, a black egg rolled out of the salmon's mouth.

The boy stamped on the egg, but his foot bounced off, and the egg didn't break. He sliced at the egg with his sword blade and hammered at the egg with the handle, but the egg didn't break.

He ran back to the girl at the mouth of the cave and gave her the black egg. She bashed

the egg against the wall of the cave, but the egg didn't break.

The boy and the girl looked at each other. They looked at the splintered tree stump and the shiny unbreakable egg.

And they heard the giant's footsteps coming back.

The boy said, "We can't break it. And he'll see the broken stump, so he'll know you've tried to get at his heart. He'll eat you tonight!"

The girl said, "No, he won't." She took off her lacy shawl. "Please cover the stump with this, as if I threw it from here."

Then she said, "I think I can guess who has to break the egg."

They heard the giant's footsteps get louder.

The boy nodded. "You're probably right. But how will we–?"

"Hide," said the girl. "Hide and leave it to me."

So the boy draped her lacy shawl over the shattered stump, and the girl put the cold, black egg under the bearskin rug at the entrance to the cave.

The giant appeared out of the trees, just as the boy hid behind the barrel.

They both watched as the giant walked into the cave, wiped his feet on the edge of the rug, then took a giant stride right over the lump in the middle.

The giant smirked at the girl. "I saw your shawl on the stump. Did you throw it on?"

"Yes, I wanted to keep your heart warm, just as the sight of you warms my heart."

He snorted. "Foolish girl."

She pulled the egg out from under the rug, held it behind her back, and walked swiftly to the middle of the cave, where she put it under the cushion on the giant's stool by the fire.

Before he sat down, the giant pulled the stool back from the heat of the fire, and the egg rolled out from under the cushion and fell toward the floor.

The girl caught it before it hit the ground.

The giant asked, "So what are you going to do next, you silly girl, knit a scarf for the deer, a hat for the duck, and nice little mittens

for the salmon's fins?" He laughed loudly.

"No," she said. "I will make crowns for them and the crowns will circle their heads like this . . ."

She put her left hand on his head and walked around him until she had her fingers on his forehead. The giant laughed at her. Then she lifted her right hand and smashed the egg as hard as she could into the thick strong bone of the giant's skull.

The egg cracked open.

And the giant fell backward off the stool, with a thump like thunder.

The giant was dead.

So the girl borrowed the boy's sword for the long and noisy job of breaking the links of her chain. Then the two of them roasted the deer, the duck, and the salmon, and shared a meal with the wolf, the hawk, and the otter.

And I don't know what happened next. Perhaps the boy and the girl decided that they made a good team, got married, and lived happily ever after together.

But it's just as likely that they shook hands, went their separate ways, and lived happily ever after on different sides of the forest.

The stories
and the sources

I love adventure stories, but I've always been disappointed that so many traditional adventure tales are about girls who need boys to save them. This led me to make radical changes to a dragon story while I was telling it to a room full of nine-year-olds, so that instead of waiting at home for a boy to kill the dragon, then being married off to him as a prize, the girl went out and killed the dragon herself (using exactly the same clever method the boy used) then refused to marry anyone. The story went down very well with the nine-year-olds, but I felt I had been unfair to the original legend. I felt I had changed the story too much, that I had ripped the heart out of it.

So since then, instead of being annoyed by the stories I know, or changing them beyond

recognition, I've been searching for authentic traditional stories with strong girls. There are lots of them out there, if you look hard enough: folktales, fairy tales, legends, and myths where the girl or goddess sorts out her own problems.

Now I am delighted to share my favorite heroine stories with you.

But I have to admit that even though I don't like to alter the heart of a story, I do often tinker with the edges, before I tell them out loud to groups of children. I might change the dialogue so it works in my voice, or fill a few plot holes so the story makes more sense to me, or add a few details so the pictures in my head are more vivid, or stretch out the chase scenes and battles to make the telling more exciting. So the stories I tell are my own versions, true to the spirit of the story which inspired me, but not identical in the words or the details. That's how stories grow and evolve and stay alive, so if you tell any of these stories, please make them your own too!

In case you want to read more about

these characters and cultures, here's where I originally found the stories. Good luck hunting for your own heroines and defeating your own monsters!

Chi and the Seven-Headed Dragon

I tell lots of dragon stories and this is one of my favorites, partly because a dragon with seven heads and 693 teeth (did you work that out?) is pretty scary and partly because Chi is a resourceful girl who kills her own dragon without help. This is my version of Sally Pomme Clayton's "Dragon Girl" story in *Amazons!* (Frances Lincoln, 2008) which is a retelling of the Chinese *Ballad of Li Chi*.

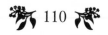

Inanna and the Box of Monsters

I love the old Sumerian myths, and the goddess Inanna has better action stories than most of the gods. The original story of Inanna and Enki, written in cuneiform writing thousands of years ago, doesn't give much detail about the monsters, so I had fun inventing the fights. However, the original does give lots of detail about the gifts, so everything Enki gives Inanna is authentically Sumerian. Even the hairdressing. I first read about Inanna in *Sumerian Mythology* by Samuel Noah Kramer (University of Pennsylvania Press, 1961) then found more recent translations online.

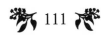

The Wolf in the Bed

I've recently written a traditional retelling of Little Red Riding Hood, which is lovely for little ones, but a bit frustrating because she has to be rescued from the wolf's belly by a man with a knife. When I was researching the origins of the tale, I found a much older version, which isn't as child-friendly, but which I really liked because the heroine saves herself. So this is my adaptation of Catherine Orenstein's translation of "The Grandmother's Tale" in *Little Red Riding Hood Uncloaked* (Basic Books, 2002).

Telesilla and the Gates of Argos

There are various versions of this story about women defending their city. I chose to adapt the one which seemed most likely and realistic to me, which is from an ancient travel guide explaining why Argos had a statue of a woman with books and a helmet: Pausanias, *Guide To Greece Volume I: Central Greece* (Penguin Classics, 1971).

Durga and the Demon

I first discovered the Hindu myth of Durga and her ten arms in *Indian Mythology* by Veronica Ions (Paul Hamlyn, 1967), then

researched many other versions to create the list of ten weapons and the variety of Mahisha's shapes which seemed most vivid and exciting to me. I'm still not sure what the lotus flower or conch shell are for, though!

Kopecho and the Two Suns

This is my expanded retelling of a tale which appears in *Yupa Folktales* by Johannes Wilbert (Latin American Center, 1974). Many old stories tell how the earth was cold and dark, and how some clever trickster found the sun to warm and light us, but I like the idea of too many suns being just as bad as no sun. I'm not sure how Kopecho managed to turn into a frog at the end though. I could have made up

a bit of plausible magic to explain it, but old stories don't always have to make complete sense!

Mbango and the Whirlpool

This is a theme which appears in stories all over the world: the downtrodden heroine is helpful and polite, and is repaid with riches, but the rude girl gets a very different reward. Most of these stories don't have pig dung in them, though, which was why I chose this one! From *An Anthology of Myths, Legends and Folktales from Cameroon* by Emmanuel Matateyou (Edwin Mellen Press, 1997).

Hervor and the Cursed Sword

I first came across Hervor in the *Encyclopedia of Goddesses and Heroines* by Patricia Monaghan (Greenwood Press, 2010), then tracked down more of her story online (including the *Saga of Hervor and King Heidrek the Wise* on http://www.northvegr. org) to create my own adaptation. But I do wonder if she made up that story about the ghosts, just to make herself seem braver. What do you think?

Visiting Baba Yaga

I found this classic witch story in *Old Peter's Russian Tales* by Arthur Ransome (Jane Nissen Books, 2003) and I've told it so often that I've probably changed it a bit. In folklore, throwing a small object behind you to create a magical obstacle is a common way to escape from a villain, and this is my favorite version of that kind of chase.

Aliquipiso and the Cliffs

There are many strong heroines in American Indian tradition, but once I'd read this story, in John Long's *Pale Moon, Tales of American*

Indians (ICS Books, 1995), I couldn't forget Aliquipiso's courage and especially her very sad end.

Tokoyo and the Skin Rope

I originally found this story (in Richard Gordon Smith's *Ancient Tales and Folklore of Japan*, A&C Black, 1918) when I was researching how long people can dive underwater for one of my adventure novels. I have to admit I've made the monster's death a bit gorier than the original, but Tokoyo's skills and bravery are the same!

The Giant's Heart

I based this story on the final part of a long tale in JF Campbell's *Popular Tales of the West Highlands Volume 1* (first published in 1860 by Edmonston and Douglas) and combined it with some elements of a very similar story in Italo Calvino's *Italian Folktales* (Penguin Books, 1982). I included this story even though the girl doesn't escape all on her own, because I like the way the boy and girl work as a team: his sword and kindness, her cleverness and courage.